Watch It Grow
Sunflower

W
FRANKLIN WATTS
LONDON•SYDNEY

First published in 2003 by Franklin Watts
96 Leonard Street, London EC2A 4XD

Franklin Watts Australia
45-51 Huntley Street, Alexandria, NSW 2015

Editor: Jackie Hamley
Art director: Jonathan Hair
Photographer: Barrie Watts
Reading consultant: Beverley Mathias

A CIP catalogue record for this book
is available from the British Library

ISBN 0 7496 4764 7

Printed in Hong Kong, China

How to use this book
Watch It Grow has been specially designed to cater for a
range of reading and learning abilities. Initially children may
just follow the pictures. Ask them to describe in their own
words what they see. Other children will enjoy reading the
single sentence in large type, in conjunction with the pictures.
This single sentence is then expanded in the main text. More
adept readers will be able to follow the text and pictures by
themselves through to the conclusion of the life cycle.

Contents

Sunflowers come from seeds.

Here is a sunflower seed. It is about 10mm long. It comes from the middle of a sunflower. The striped coating is hard and tough. It stops the inside parts of the seed from drying out.

Inside the seed is a store of food that will be used to grow a new plant. During the winter the seed is kept in a cool, dry place until it is ready to be planted.

The seed is planted.

In spring, when the weather becomes warmer, the seed is planted in soil. The seed needs warmth and water to start to grow.

A week after planting, the coating of the seed has softened. Water from the soil gets through the coating. As it gets wet, the inside of the seed swells. The coating then splits open.

The seed grows roots.

Soon after the soft seed coating splits open, a tiny root pushes its way out.

The root grows down into the soil.
It collects water and **nutrients**,
which are sent back to the seed.

The seed leaves grow.

As the root sends water and **nutrients** back to the seed, the first leaves, called **seed leaves**, start to grow. They grow on top of a tube, called the stem.

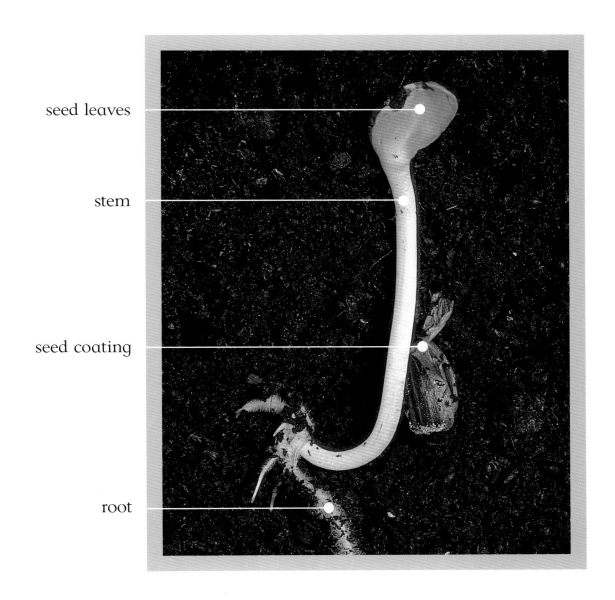

seed leaves

stem

seed coating

root

The **seed leaves** push their way to the surface of the soil. They are folded downwards as they force their way up through the soil, so that they do not get damaged.

The seed leaves are big.

As soon as the **seed leaves** reach the surface of the soil, they unfold. They are oval and have a different shape from a normal leaf. The **seed leaves** use sunlight to start making food for the plant.

The food gives the plant the energy
it needs to grow. Now it can push
its roots deep into the soil. The
more roots the plant has, the more
water and **nutrients** it will get,
and the quicker it will grow.

The proper leaves grow.

A week after the **seed leaves** appear, the sunflower plant's proper leaves start to grow. They grow big, up to 30cm long. The proper leaves use sunlight to make even more food.

The proper leaves have a network of thin, hollow tubes, called **veins**. These **veins** carry food to the rest of the plant. When the proper leaves have grown, the **seed leaves** are no longer needed. They go yellow and dry up.

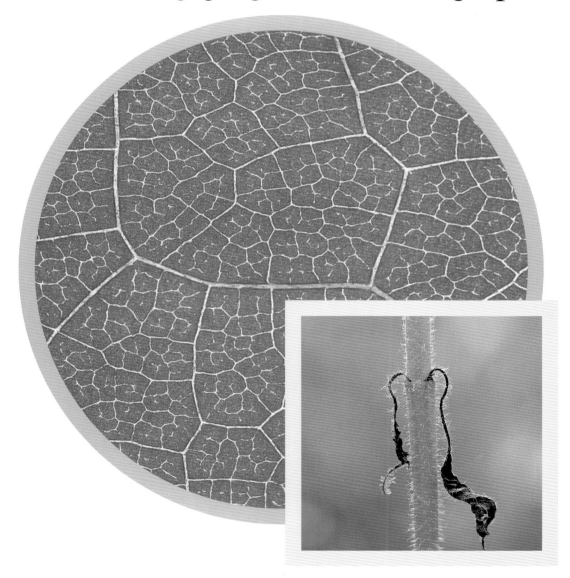

The stem is strong.

The stem
of the plant joins
the roots and the leaves. It is a tube
filled with soft, sponge-like **veins**
which carry food and water to the
other parts of the sunflower plant.

The stem can grow to over 2 metres high and is very strong and flexible. It supports the plant as it grows upwards and, later, its heavy flower.

The flower starts to grow.

After two months, the sunflower plant has grown several large leaves. These make lots of food so the plant can start to grow a flower bud.

The flower bud grows at the tip of
the stem, where the newest leaves
appear. At first, only the outer parts
of the flower can be seen.

The flower bud is big.

Before the bud opens, it is covered with thin, pointed green scales. These are the **sepals** of the flower. The **sepals** protect the soft parts of the flower as they grow inside the bud.

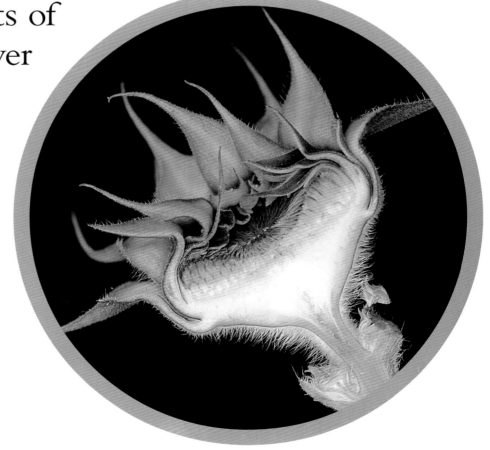

The **sepals** are tough and hairy. They stop insects from eating the flower before it opens. When it is fully grown, the flower bud is as big as a chicken's egg.

The sunflower opens.

The flower opens on a warm, sunny day. It takes at least a day to open fully. Unlike many other flowers, a sunflower has both male and female parts in each flower head.

After four days, the male parts start to make **pollen**, and the female parts, called **stigmas**, make **nectar**. The **nectar** smells sweet and attracts insects. The bright yellow colour also tempts insects to visit the sunflower.

The sunflower faces the sun.

Most sunflowers grow in warm, sunny parts of the world, often in large fields. Each sunflower is about 30cm across.

The big flowers need the warm
sunlight to make **nectar**, so each
flower turns to face the sun.
In a large field, all the sunflowers
will face the sun. They slowly follow
it as it moves across the sky.

Insects visit the sunflower.

Bees, flies, crickets and other insects visit the sunflower to feed on the sweet **nectar**. When they land on the flower, they get covered in sticky **pollen** from the male parts of the flower.

The insects carry the **pollen** to other sunflowers. As the insects land on the female **stigmas**, **pollen** brushes off them and the **stigmas** are **fertilised**. When this happens, a seed begins to grow.

The sunflower makes seeds.

When all the female **stigmas** have been **fertilised**, the flower is no longer needed. Its petals dry up. The flower head hangs downwards to stop rain from harming the growing seeds.

The plant keeps making food which is stored in the growing seeds. By autumn, they are ready to **harvest**. Some seeds will be eaten or crushed to make oil. Others will be planted next spring to grow new sunflowers.

Word bank

Fertilised - The female parts of a sunflower are fertilised when they come into contact with pollen from the male parts of a sunflower. This happens when insects move between sunflowers. Only a fertilised sunflower will make seeds.

Harvest - When people collect fully-grown crops from fields or gardens.

Nectar - A sweet liquid made by the female parts of a sunflower. Nectar attracts bees and other insects.

Nutrients - Substances in the soil that help plants to grow.

Pollen - A fine powder made by the male parts of a sunflower that fertilises the female parts.

Seed leaves - The first leaves that grow on a plant before the proper leaves grow.

Sepals - The outside part of a flower which protects the petals as they grow inside the flower bud.

Stigmas - The female parts of a flower that make nectar. When a stigma is fertilised by pollen, a seed starts to grow.

Veins - The tiny tubes in a leaf or in the stem that carry food and water around the plant.

Life cycle

Soon after planting, a root from the sunflower seed pushes down into the soil.

When the sunflower is fertilised it makes seeds. Next spring, these can be planted to grow new sunflowers.

A few days later, the stem and seed leaves grow.

Soon after opening, the sunflower makes nectar. This attracts insects.

The seed leaves push to the surface and unfold.

About four weeks later, the sunflower opens.

A week later, the proper leaves grow.

After eight weeks the plant starts to grow a flower bud.

Index